MEDITATIONS™ WITH DANTE ALIGHIERI

Introduction and Versions by

James Collins

Bear & Company
Santa Fe, New Mexico

Cover Illustration:

"THE DARK WOOD" by H. J. Nawn
"Halfway along the journey of our life, having strayed from
the right path and lost it, I awoke to find myself in a
dark wood. . . I soon came to the bottom of a hill where the
valley that had impaled my heart with terror came to an end.
I looked high up the hill and could see its back already
clad in the rays of that star which guides other men along
the proper way."

Bear & Company Books are published by Bear & Company, Inc. Its Trademark, consisting of the words "Bear & Company" and the portrayal of a
bear, is Registered in U.S. Patent and Trademark Office and in other countries. Marca Registrada Bear & Company, Inc., P.O. Drawer 2860, Santa
Fe, New Mexico 87504.

Meditations With™ and the representation thereof, is registered in U.S.
Patent and Trademark Office and in other countries. Marca Registrada,
Bear & Company, Inc., P.O. Drawer 2860, Santa Fe, New Mexico 87504.

ISBN 0-939680-18-1

Library of Congress Card Number 84-072256

Typography: Casa Sin Nombre, Santa Fe

Illustrations: Harry J. Nawn

Printed in the United States by BookCrafters

WHAT IS THE MEDITATIONS WITH ™ SERIES?

Bear & Co. is publishing this series of creation-centered mystic/prophets to bring to the attention and prayer of peoples today the power and energy of the holistic mystics of the western tradition. One reason western culture succumbs to boredom and to violence is that we are not being challenged by our religious traditions to be all we can be. This is also the reason that many sincere spiritual seekers go East for their mysticism — because the West is itself out of touch with its deepest spiritual guides. The format Bear & Co. has chosen in which to present these holistic mystic/prophets is deliberate: We do not feel that more academically-styled books on our mystics is what every-day believers need: Rather, we wish to get the mystics of personal and social transformation off our dusty shelves and into the hearts and minds and bodies of our people. To do this we choose a format that is ideal for meditation, for imaging, for sharing in groups and in prayer occasions. We rely on primary sources for the texts but we let the author's words and images flow from her or his inner structure to our deep inner selves.

Introduction

As I begin this introduction I am looking at children playing on the beach at Cape May Point in New Jersey. The child in me comes alive as I see small children on the seashore: how they delight in the powerful, yet playful, waves! The ocean is a big playmate to them that never tires of playing "rough and tumble" with them. The children also delight in the many small living creatures they discover at the ocean's edge: sand crabs, clams, and mussels. They find pretty shells—serendipity everywhere! They chase the sandpipers that constantly elude them.

This is a fresh, fascinating world for children, especially for those who have lived in crowded, dirty cities and then have their first encounter with the seashore. The delights of this new world fill them with laughter, surprise, and *joie de vivre*. The beauty and charm of this new discovery totally capture their attention, interest, and love.

It seems to me that Dante Alighieri records a somewhat similar experience of his own childhood when he describes his meeting in 1274 with a young girl named Beatrice when he and she were only nine years old. The delight of this first encounter remained with him all his life, but its profound meaning unfolded to him only later when he was in his middle years. The impression was so strong and vivid that it had remained indelible. It was a vision of pure beauty, but more importantly, it was a first taste of the experience we call love.

Dante tells the story of this meeting in his charming book, *La Vita Nuova*, a work which might be translated as *My Young Life*, since the expression *vita nuova* in Dante's terminology meant one's youth. The book is not autobiographical in the ordinary sense of the word, but is more like a meditation on the history of his soul's awakening to love. It actually became the preface to a much more lengthy spiritual journal: his *Comedy*. But this little work already expresses in embryonic form the deep intuition Dante had in his youth of the meaning of life, of love, of his own soul, and of God. All of these were inseparably intertwined for Dante throughout his life.

To the superficial reader of *La Vita Nuova* the work may appear to be just another outpouring of a sentimental lover hopelessly searching to console himself for the loss of his beloved. That type of love poetry was "all the rage" in Dante's time. The Italian poets consciously imitated the troubador style of love poetry which had developed in *La Provence* and spread throughout Europe. Dante, however, radically transformed that love poetry by transcending the narrow limits of the troubadours' poetic and romantic sighs. Many troubadours, under pressure from the Church's dim view of an exclusive, all-absorbing love and adoration of a creature, often spent their last days in monasteries repenting of their ill-spent youth and talents, particularly their "idolatrous" devotion to a human creature.

Dante successfully overcame that conflict of "good love" (for God alone) and "bad love" (for the creature), which had become so characteristic of Western medieval piety. That conflict no doubt had its roots in the widespread Neo-platonic dichotomy of spirit/flesh which flourished through the writings of the Fathers of the Church, particularly St. Augustine. Although Dante was strongly influenced by that Augustinian mindset, he nonetheless subtly, yet unequivocally, avoided the pitfalls of that either/or choice in the objects of one's love.

Dante, influenced more by the spiritual vision of St. Francis of Assisi and St. Bonaventure, loved both God *and* God's creatures with one ecstatic burst of joy. He embraced the creature with complete abandon, knowing that at the same time He was embracing the Creator. For Dante, God is in the creature and the creature is in God. This "panentheism," as we often call it today, was a hallmark of Francis' spirituality as it was also of the spirituality of many medieval mystics such as Mechtild of Magdeburg, Hildegard of Bingen, Meister Eckhart, to name only a few. We might say that it was a recovery of the biblical insight that God is in fact present in God's creation.

In the *Vita Nuova*, Dante centers his attention on one particular individual of God's creation: a young woman named Beatrice Portinari. She, the real "flesh and blood" girl whom Dante knew and loved in Florence in the late thirteenth century, was for Dante the living revelation of God's loving presence in his life. He lavished such extravagant praises on her that when his *Vita Nuova* was first printed in the sixteenth century, the narrow-minded clergymen of the time found Dante's praises of Beatrice to be sacrilegious and even blasphemous. According to the ecclesiastical critics, Dante had attributed to Beatrice words and phrases that should be reserved only for God or Christ. Dante's work could be published only in ecclesiastically expurgated editions.

The benighted clerics had clearly misunderstood the entire gist of Dante's spirituality. They had failed to appreciate the very foundation of Dante's sacramental and incarnational theology, namely that Beatrice was a concrete, particular manifestation—a sacrament—of God's loving presence in the world. They had lost the basic vision of Jesus, who said that his sisters and brothers in this world were indeed to be identified with him. "What you do to the least of my brethren, you do to me" was apparently not taken seriously by those sixteenth century *censores librorum*. They had misinterpreted Dante's profound understanding of the analogy between Creator and creature because they had lost sight of the marvelous Good News proclaimed by Jesus that God is present in the particular persons and things which God creates.

Dante, then, in exalting and loving the particular person Beatrice, was simply living out the Gospel. He perceived in the particular the wonderful, mysterious presence of God. That was not a source of scandal for Dante but rather a cause for joy, love, thanksgiving, and praise. Dante was literally compelled and inspired to express his love: his love for Beatrice and simultaneously his love for God. In his *Vita Nuova* he recounts how love was first awakened in his soul at the sight of the human creature Beatrice. This apparently ordinary attraction and thrill—human *eros*—was the beginning and spark of a great flame which developed into the brilliance and white heat of divine *agape*, expressed so passionately later in the *Divine Comedy*. Even in his earlier work the seed, the profound insight, was dimly present. It took a lifetime, however, for that seed to germinate into the transcendent beauty of the white rose of Paradise.

In his lifetime Dante made many detours and wandered far from that initial, childlike vision of love. He was sidetracked by the distractions of fame, passions, disappointment, frustrations, and exile: enemies within himself and outside himself. Dante was no stranger to the experience we commonly call the "dark night of the soul." He devoted a third of his *Comedy*—the *Inferno*—to a ruthless description of that state of misery.

Even though Dante tasted the bitter dregs of misery in his own life, he was not a dreary person nor was he an angry, embittered man. Unfortunately the popular image of Dante even today is the stern, gloomy reformer and author of the *Inferno*, the somber judge of sinful humanity. Although he exhibited all the fiery passion of a reformer because of his intense, restless pursuit of justice, he was first and last a man of compassion, humor, and tender love. His writings—if one troubles to read beyond the *Inferno*—reveal a poet of the most delicate sensitivity, a prophet who speaks a desperately needed message to his world, and a mystic whose love of God and God's creation was as deep and real as that of any of the recognized mystics of Christian history.

If Dante has appeared to the public as an outside observer and judge of his world it is because the world of his time relegated him to such a position on the fringe of established society. The "powers that were" (mainly the Church's authority vested in the political, corrupt popes of his time) could not tolerate such an outspoken critic and champion of justice and peace. Dante, a layman and an elected official in the complex politics of Florence, was a fearless opponent of papal military power, greed, and corruption. As a result he was condemned to permanent exile and death by burning if he had ever returned to Florence. His twenty-some years of wandering through Italy in search of hospitality proved to be a blessing in disguise: it was in those years, in that painful separation from his native city, his family, and friends, that Dante created his monumental masterpiece, the *Divine Comedy.* His poetic, theological, and mystical gifts developed and reached maturity through exile and suffering. The gold was refined in the fire of pain and deprivation, and we are the fortunate and grateful heirs of that fine gold.

It seems to be the old story of the phoenix rising from its ashes, and indeed it is: it's the ageless pattern of the Jewish exodus from slavery to freedom; it's the way lovingly accepted by Jesus in his suffering, death, and resurrection. It is the paschal mystery relived in the Middle Ages, in Dante's own life. He begins his journey through Hell on Good Friday and emerges from the pit on Easter Sunday. The story of his soul is the story of the ancient Jews, of Jesus, of every Christian who dies and is reborn by God's gratuitous love.

This story—ever ancient and ever new—will be the subject of these meditations. They will follow the four-fold path of Meister Eckhart's spirituality, as outlined and explained by Matthew Fox. This method will in no way impose a foreign or artificial pattern on Dante's own spiritual journey. Dante and Eckhart were in fact contemporaries and both were heirs to a well-established spirituality, even though both were highly original, creative thinkers and writers. It is no surprise that we discover a basically similar pattern of spiritual development in both of these intellectual and mystical giants.

The first step in the spiritual journey according to Eckhart is creation. Dante's own spiritual odyssey begins with his encounter with Beatrice, who is for him the God-bearing image, the sacrament of

God's creative love for him. In the first part of these meditations the passages will be taken mainly from Dante's youthful work, *La Vita Nuova*. The springtime freshness of first love and the childlike wonder and delight of Dante's love for Beatrice are the focus of that work. This is clearly the *via positiva*, the affirmation of God's gifts.

This positive way affirms that the human person is a mirror of God's beauty: the human reflects and contains divine grace and is a vehicle and sacrament of God's creative activity in the world here and now. Created nature is in itself graced with God's presence and love. Beatrice is an incarnation of that created grace and Dante's exuberant praise of Beatrice is at the same time praise of the Creator of such grace.

In the second phase of these meditations the focus will be on the first part of Dante's *Comedy*, the *Inferno*. There Dante explores the *via negativa*, the brutal forces within his own soul and every human soul which turn the soul away from the vision and enjoyment of God and God's gifts. He describes this experience as a detour into a dark forest populated with ravenous beasts which prevent the soul from reaching the Mount of Joy, where the earthly paradise, mankind's true home, is found. The journey into Hell is a descent into the dark, negative caverns of the human soul: its deadly passions and sins, which hold the soul captive and lost to its real life and activity.

Dante there learns that sin is the ugly perversion of the soul's ability to love. It is a kind of gradual sclerosis of the heart which ends in a frozen immobility, the lowest pit of Hell where evil is gruesomely personified in Satan, who presides over his immobile world of ice: the very perversion of God's creative love, which is a warm, life-giving flow of God's own goodness. Dante's *Inferno* is anything but a self-righteous gloating over the punishments of his contemporaries. Contrary to popular misconceptions, Dante does not play the vindictive observer who delights in finding his enemies suffering their just deserts. He is more interested in probing the causes of human misery—his own and society's—in order to know the enemy within, which prevents us from attaining the happiness for which God created us.

The third stage of these meditations will center on Dante's *Purgatorio*, his ascent of the mountain which is crowned with the earthly paradise. This is truly a "breakthrough" from the infernal prison and a liberation from the negative forces of sin. It is the *via creativa*, the creative path, where Dante is recreated by God's grace into the beautiful divine image. Dante becomes free and light, as the heaviness of sin is gradually lifted from him. His true self becomes transparent to him as a result of the arduous climb. When he finally arrives at the bright, divine forest he becomes like a child again, full of wonder, innocence, and love.

There he encounters the woman Matelda, who personifies Dante's newly acquired innocence. Many Dante scholars believe the woman to be Mechtild of Magdeburg. It is very likely that Dante knew her writings, which had been translated into Latin during her lifetime. She represents the newborn soul of Dante which rejoices in the goodness of God's creation. She is the one who baptizes Dante and leads him to Beatrice, who arrives in a blaze of glory similar to the second coming of Christ. The pilgrim at last finds his lost love, the woman who images forth God's glorious, creative love.

Dante's journey, however, is not yet at an end. Beatrice is not the final goal of his pilgrimage. She leads him into the heavenly paradise, which is the subject of the last part of the *Comedy*. Excerpts from the *Paradiso* will be the content of the last part of these meditations. Paradise is the *via transformativa:* the tragedy of human misery is completely transformed into a divine comedy. In the *Paradiso* Dante, who had already been made whole and free, becomes transformed and divinized. He experiences new, unexpected dimensions of his being as he soars with Beatrice into the glory of God. The experience of Paradise is cosmic ecstasy. Dante describes it in many ways; "the laughter of the universe" is one such poetic description.

In Paradise Dante meets old friends, relatives, famous saints and sinners of history, who are all absorbed in one eternal song and dance motivated by mutual love. They are all attuned to and caught up in the one love which binds them all together in one joyous activity: a revelling in God's love for them. Having found their true center and home, they are totally transformed into bright lights while still maintaining their individual personalities. God's love shines through them and fills them with ecstatic joy. Dante joins in this marvelous experience and feels his entire being moving with that same movement which emanates from the First Mover—God, who is love. Dante's God is no static, abstract "first unmoved mover" of Aristotle's philosophy, but rather a personal source of all movement and life, since God is love itself.

Dante in this ultimate experience receives a mission to transmit this experience to earth in order that the world too may escape its insane, tragic misery of injustice and greed and be transformed by the vision of the *real* reality: God's constant love for creation, God's overflowing compassion, and peace. Dante's extraordinary vision of Paradise is not some sort of reward for his good life or ascetical practices. It is a grace freely granted to a pilgrim/sinner; it is a message which could save a world immersed in greed and selfish pride, a world blindly headed toward its own destruction. Perhaps a distant mirror of our twentieth century?

Dante's *Paradiso* then is not some grandiose boast about an exceptional mystical experience, but rather a prophetic word given to transform a world which had lost its way and had perverted its God-given destiny. The experience of Paradise is not an escape from the problems of this world; it *is* a vision of the universe with God as its center and love as the only vital force which keeps it all together in peace and harmony. It is a re-discovery of true sanity, which is really an ecstatic experience of entering into the oneness of God and the universe.

Paradise should be construed not so much as a place "out there"— just as Hell and Purgatory are not primarily places "out there." Dante, assuming the real existence of such "places" or "states" beyond this world, is mainly describing the inner landscape of the human soul which by choice can be a hell of fiercely negative drives, a purgatory of continuous growth and rebirth, or a paradise of love and ecstatic joy.

Dante reveals to us the choices which God freely gives us, but he also proclaims with the conviction of faith that God's will is for our peace and happiness.

Since the passages in this book of meditations are extracted from the context of Dante's own spiritual pilgrimage, they must be understood and appropriated by each of us in our own individual way. Dante explicitly declares at the beginning of his *Comedy* that he is writing about "our journey." He invites each of us to make the pilgrimage with him. We can journey with him even in spite of the differences of times and circumstances. His experience of Beatrice can be interpreted by us in the context of our own lives: she may be a wonderful person whom we love; she may be God's creation in all its totality or some particular aspect—the flowers or animals, the sea or the mountains, the sunset or the moon. Our imagination can translate Dante's images, which were everyday, particular realities to him, into the everyday persons and things we encounter today. In that way these meditations can speak to us today and lead us into the real experience of prayer—a joyful, ecstatic celebration of our oneness with and in God.

In my translation of Dante's writings, I have sometimes taken some liberties, which I hope do not compromise Dante's meaning. At times my rendition departs noticeably from Dante's literal text in order to summarize or clarify for the modern reader the sense of a particular passage. This method of paraphrasing Dante often enters the realm of interpretation, as all translations necessarily do; but I have relied for the most part on the current interpretations of respected Dantean scholars. I trust that I have not betrayed Dante's deepest purposes in my rather liberal approach to the original text.

James Collins
Holy Family College
Torresdale, Pennsylvania

H. J. Nawn   *Beatrice*

PATH I.   BEGINNING THE JOURNEY:
Gazing with love on God's Creation

God,
the Supreme Goodness,
breathes forth your soul directly
and falls in love with you,
so that from then on you always desire God.

God's Goodness,
burning within Itself,
sends forth sparks
and unfolds Its eternal beauties.
These sparks, human souls,
which come directly from God,
have no end:
they are imprinted forever
with the stamp of God's beauty.

The human soul issues from the hands of God,
Who loves her even before she is created.
She is like a playful little child,
laughing and weeping.
The simple soul,
who knows nothing
except that she is animated by a happy Maker,
turns willingly toward whatever delights her.

Gaze lovingly upon the art
of that supreme Artist
whose loving eyes
never turn away from it.

Just as we see little children
intensely longing for an apple,
and then going on further
longing for a little bird,
and further on desiring fine clothes,
and later a horse and then a lover,
we perceive that the human soul
never finds what she is ever searching for:
the supreme good, God.

A pilgrim
traveling on a road where he has never been
    before
believes every house he sees from afar is the inn;
and not finding it, directs his belief to another;
and so from house to house
until he comes to the inn.
In the same way our soul,
as soon as she begins
the new, never yet made, journey of life,
directs her eyes
toward the goal of her supreme good
and whatever she sees
that appears to have some good in it
she thinks to be *it*.

At the first sight of Beatrice
my spirit spoke to me these words:
Your happiness has now appeared to you!
From that moment love mastered my soul
and held so much sway
that the powers of my imagination
completely surrendered to it.
Her beauty was so noble
and worthy of praise
that I could say of her:
She seemed not the daughter of a mortal man
but of God!

Love,
not because of my goodness (which is so meagre),
but out of its own nobleness
made my life so sweet and calm
that I heard people say of me:
What a worthy and fortunate man
to have such a happy heart!

Whenever Beatrice appeared
no enemy was present to me,
but rather a flame of love possessed me
which made me forgive all who had offended me.
When asked about my new attitude,
my answer would simply be: Love!

Love said to me:
I am like the center of a circle
to which are related
all the points of its circumference.

Love says of her:
How can something mortal be so lovely
    and pure?
God intends to create in her
what never yet was created.
She is the utmost that Nature
can create of goodness.
By her example
beauty is proved to be real.

From her eyes dart out flaming spirits of love
which strike the eyes of him who looks on them.
These flames touch and pierce to the heart.
You see love painted on her smile,
which no one can gaze on steadfastly.

Love and a gentle heart
are one and the same thing.
The one without the other
can no more exist
than a rational soul without reason.

My lady bears love in her eyes.
Anyone she looks on becomes gentle.
Wherever she passes
everyone turns to her
and she makes the heart of everyone
     whom she greets
tremble.

The one who ponders carefully
would call Beatrice *love*
because of the great similarity she has to love.

When this most gentle lady passes by,
many say: This is a marvel,
and blessed be the Lord
Who knows how to work such wonders!

The one who sees my lady
sees perfectly all saving power.
Those who go with her
give thanks to God for God's beautiful grace.

Her beauty is of such power
that others are not filled with envy,
but rather become clothed in
humility, love and faith.
The sight of her makes everyone humble;
and not only makes her seem lovely,
but each one through her receives honor.
Her bearing is so gentle
that no one who calls her to mind
can help sighing with the sweetness of love.

The number nine was her very self.
The analogy which I understand by this number
can be explained in this way:
since three times three make nine,
and three is the sole factor of nine,
and the sole factor of miracles is three
—the Father, Son and Holy Spirit,
Who are three in one—
this lady was a nine,
a miracle whose root
is the wonderful Trinity alone.

My pilgrim soul
yearns to look on my departed lady
who now shines in glory and splendor.

If it be the pleasure of God
by Whom all things live,
that my life endure for some few years,
I hope to write of her
what has never been written of any woman.
And then may it please God Who is Lord of grace
that my soul go and behold
the glory of its lady, the Blessed Beatrice,
who gazes in glory on the face of God
Who is Blessed forever.

H. J. Nawn *Purgatory*

PATH II.   THE DETOUR:
Becoming Lost in the Dark Forest

Midway in the journey of our life
I found myself in a dark forest
for I had lost the straight path.

Oh how hard it is to tell
what a wild, rugged, and harsh forest this was!
The very thought of it renews my fear.

So terrible it is that death is hardly worse.
But to reveal the good that I found in it,
I will tell of the things I saw there.

The day was Good Friday
and the time was the beginning of morning.
The sun was rising with those stars
that were with it when Divine Love
first set those beautiful things in motion.

The hour of the day
and the sweet season of Spring
gave me cause for good hope
in spite of the terrifying beasts
that confronted me:
the leopard of lust,
the lion of pride,
and the wolf of greed,
the fiercest of the three.

The sight of these beasts
instilled such fear and distress in me
that I lost hope of ascending
the bright mountain of joy in the distance.
Little by little,
I was driven down to where the sun is silent.

The wolf of greed is so vicious and perverse
that it never satisfies its greedy desires,
and after feeding is hungrier than before.

Many are the beasts with which it mates,
and there will yet be more
until the Hound, the Holy Spirit,
shall come and deal it a painful death.
He will not feed on land or money,
but on wisdom, love and strength.
This Savior will hunt it through every town
until God has driven it back to Hell
whence envy first sent it forth.

The thought of a journey into Hell
to confront these evil beasts within me
caused terror at first.
As my courage collapsed,
an inner guide, my reason,
reassured me
that a splendid heavenly lady was supporting
me
and encouraging me to make the hard journey.

She spoke these words:

> My friend, I am Beatrice,
> who direct you to go.
> Love moved me and makes me speak.
> There is a gentle Lady in heaven, Mary,
> who has pity on you.
> She, as well as your patron saint Lucy,
> sent me to rescue you
> as you flounder in the river of evil,
> the most terrible of seas.
> We three ladies are living channels
> of God's loving care for you.
> What then is holding you back?
> Why does fear keep your heart
> from being bold and free?

As little flowers,
bent over and closed by the night chill,
straighten up and open again on their stems,
when the sun returns to warm and shine on them.

So I revived my failing strength
and so much courage rushed into my heart
that I responded like someone set free:

O compassionate Lady,
you give me the help I need.
Your words give my heart the strength
to start on the deep, wild journey
into the dark, terrifying caverns of evil.

Hell, I discovered,
is the woeful loss of our highest good, God.
The three Divine Persons,
Who are Power, Wisdom and Love,
became absent when we deliberately abandon
their path of justice and love.
The misery and pain of Hell
is our turning away from Them
to follow misleading banners
of ego-worship and indifference.
Such standards blind us
to anyone or anything outside ourselves.
They lead us to a total refusal to love unselfishly,
the ultimate vacuum of despair and misery.

In the first circle of Hell
the lustful, the least malicious,
are driven aimlessly by the infernal storm.
They are restless since they subjected
their reason to passionate desires.

They have no hope of repose
as they lament and blame their plight on "love."
They were in love with love,
rather than with the other and "The Other."

In a lower region of Hell are the greedy,
who competed ruthlessly with one another
for the goods of the world.
They either recklessly consumed things
or hoarded them for the future.

Greed still tears the human race apart
and pits one person against another,
nation against nation.
What insanity and blindness!
All the gold
that is under the moon or ever was
cannot give rest to a single human soul.

Greedy souls
blame and curse Fortune for their misery.
Fortune,
the wise lady who administers divine providence,
transfers wealth mysteriously from nation
        to nation,
from one family to another.
We do not understand her hidden designs.

Near the dismal bottom of the hellish pit,
where evil is at its worst,
are the traitors,
frozen to their waist in an icy lake.
Their only activity
is a relentless violence against one another.

Weeping there prevents them from weeping:
the tears find a barrier in their eyes,
which are covered with an icy visor.
The tears turn inward to increase the pain.

One cruel soul there
continues his earthly treachery
by gnawing on the skull of his victim,
as a dog would chew his bone.
Treacherous souls
are locked into their refusal to love.
They continue to choose themselves
over anything or anyone else.
Their pitiless arrogance is the horror of Hell.

At the very bottom
and dead end of the dark pit of Hell,
Satan is frozen in the center of the lake.
The once beautiful "Light-Bearer,"
the most noble of God's creatures,
is now the monstrous source of evil.

The hideous nature of pride,
and of all sins,
is depicted on Satan's three deformed faces.
One is sallow from moral decay;
another is black from ignorance;
the third is blood-red from rage.
The three faces are a perverse parody
of the three Divine Persons:
Power, Wisdom and Love.

Satan's three mouths
eternally devour three infamous traitors
who turned against their friends and benefactors.
They are Judas Iscariot, who betrayed Jesus;
Brutus and Cassius, who betrayed Julius Caesar.
The essence of sin
is betrayal of the one who loves us.
This refusal to love
is what chills and hardens
the human heart created to love.
This is the ultimate perversion
of God's good creation:
the creature's proud rebellion against
     God's good plan.

Satan's gloomy realm,
located in the pit of the earth,
is directly below Jerusalem,
the center of the upper world
and place where God's Son shed God's blood
on Good Friday.
His sacrificial love
generated life, warmth and light for the world.
Satan's reign produces
only hatred, paralysis, darkness and ice.

After this horrendous glimpse of evil
I emerged at the other side
of the earth's sphere
to behold once again the bright, beautiful stars.
It was Easter morning and the time to rise.

H. J. Nawn　　*Hell*

PATH III.　THE BREAKTHROUGH:
Recreating the Divine Image Within Us

Now the little vessel of my soul
hoists her sails to move on to better waters,
leaving behind a sea so cruel.

I will sing of the second realm,
Purgatory,
where the human spirit cleanses itself
and becomes worthy of the ascent to see God.

A sweet color of oriental sapphire,
which was gathering in the serene face of the sky,
restored delight to my eyes
as soon as I came out of the dead air
that had afflicted my eyes and lungs.

The beautiful planet Venus,
that moves one to love,
made the whole East smile.
The sky rejoiced in her light.

After the painful sight of sin's ravages,
I was now ready to see
how human souls cleanse themselves
and make themselves beautiful and free.

I found myself on a little island,
which is a seven-story mountain.
At the base of the mountain,
I washed my tear-stained face
from the infernal filth
and clothed myself with a green reed
plucked from the shore.

The dawn was dispelling the morning darkness,
which fled before her.
The light trembled on the sea
as the cheeks of the beautiful dawn
changed from white, to rosy, to bright orange.

A sudden light darted across the waters.
It was God's angel,
ferrying the blessed souls
across the sea to the island.
They were singing joyfully
the ancient Passover psalm:
"When Israel made her exodus out of Egypt."
I joined the newly arrived pilgrims
for the joyful climb of the mountain.

The souls of these new pilgrims were like sheep,
simple and timid.
But one of them came forward from that happy
    flock.
He had been excommunicated by popes,
killed in battle with papal forces,
but had entrusted himself to God's mercy
as he died, He spoke:

> Horrible were my sins,
> but Infinite Goodness
> has wide, open arms,
> embracing who turn to It.

> If the earthly shepherd had read that page,
> the merciful face of God,
> he would not have buried me dishonorably
> with quenched tapers.

> By ecclesiastical curse no one is so lost
> that Eternal Love cannot come to him
> as long as hope bears a green leaf.

The climb up the mountains was at first very
    hard,
but the higher one goes, the easier it becomes.

My guide, Virgil, assured me
that the ascent would become as easy
as floating in a boat down a stream.
Power from Heaven comes to those
who seek to scale the mountain.

It was now the hour of sunset
when those far off at sea long for their homes.
Their hearts tenderly think of the day
when they bid farewell to their sweet friends.

The hour pierces the new pilgrim's heart
with love when he hears the distant church bells
which seem to mourn the dying day.

I watched one of the spirits
who lifted his hands and gazed on the East,
as if saying to God:
"For nothing else do I care!"

He then intoned the vesper hymn,
"Before the close of day,
Creator of the world, we pray."
The sweet notes made me unconscious
of everything else,
and I too became rapt
in a nostalgic longing for God.

On the first terrace of Purgatory
I moved along side by side with the souls
purifying their sin of pride.
They were bent over almost to the ground
as they carried heavy stones.

Pride makes us so miserable and weary
because it distorts our mental vision.
It prevents us from being aware
that we are now only worms,
yet destined to form the angelic butterfly
that will soar defenseless to God.
Vain pride makes our minds swell
so that we forget
that presently we are still imperfect and
        incomplete
like caterpillars
whose full development is yet to come.

On the mountainside of the first terrace
I saw carved in marble
examples of humility to spur us on to imitation.
The first image showed Mary
humbly responding to the angel Gabriel:
"Behold the handmaid of the Lord."

With those words she received the decree of
peace,
wept for during so many years,
which opened Heaven from its long interdict.
Her humility was the key that opened God's love.

Then I saw an image of King David,
flinging away his regal robes
and dancing wildly before the Ark of the
      Covenant.
He forgot himself and his royal dignity
as he praised the Lord.

The souls learning humility
pray with words based on the Lord's prayer:

Our Father, Who are in Heaven,
not restricted there, but through greater love
    for Your first creatures,
the angels,

May Your name and Your power
be praised by every creature,
since it is fitting to give thanks
for Your sweet out-pouring of goodness.

May the peace of Your reign come to us,
for we cannot attain it by ourselves,
with all our efforts,
unless it comes from You.

Just as Your angels sacrifice their will to You,
singing hosannas,
so may humans do with theirs.

Give us today our daily manna,
without which we would only go backwards
in this harsh desert,
if we tried to advance.

As we forgive others
for the evil we have endured,
may You in Your loving-kindness forgive us;
and do not consider our just desserts.

Do not test our strength,
which is so easily overcome
by the old adversary;
but deliver us from him
who so spurs us to evil.

This last petition, dear Lord,
we make not for ourselves,
for we do not need it,
but for those who remain behind us.

On the second storey of the mountain,
the souls cleanse themselves of envy,
the sin which, rooted in pride,
blinds us to the existence and needs of others.
This selfishness
sets human hearts on material things
and leads them to exclude
the common sharing of those things.

The ineffable and infinite good,
shares itself
just as a ray of light
rushes to a bright surface
expands and fills it.

In the same way,
a good thing divided among many
makes each far richer
than if it were possessed only by a few.
The greater the number
who embrace and love each other,
the more love there is,
since one gives to another,
just as the light expands itself on the mirror.

The sin of wrath is purged
on the third ledge of Purgatory,
where the souls learn forgiveness
by contemplating the image of Stephen,
the first Christian martyr.
In the image a crowd,
burning with rage,
is stoning the youthful Stephen
as they shout: "Kill! Kill!"

Stephen is sinking to the earth,
but his eyes open Heaven
as he prays to God in his agony.
With a look that unlocks pity
he forgives his persecutors
just as Jesus on the cross had forgiven His.

The souls then untie their knot of anger
by singing "Lamb of God"
in complete harmony.

The fourth ledge,
where the sin of sloth is cleansed,
is the place for delay
since the souls who were slow to love
must pause to learn the meaning of love.
Virgil gives this profound insight
into the nature of love:

> Neither Creator nor creature
> was ever without love,
> whether it was instinctive
> or dependent on the will.

The instinctive is always without error,
but the other can err through an evil object,
or through too much or too little vigor.
While it is directed to the Prime Good
and is moderate in other things,
it cannot be the cause of sinful pleasure.

But when it turns to evil or speeds to good
with too much or too little zeal,
the creature works against its creator.

Hence you can understand
that love is the seed of every virtue in you
and of every sinful action as well.

Since love can never turn
from the welfare of its possessor,
all creatures are free from self-hatred.

It follows
that the evil we love is our neighbor's;
and this arises in three ways in our human nature:

Some—the proud—hoping to excel,
long only to reduce the greatness of their
neighbors.
Others—the envious—fear losing power,
honor and fame if another rises;
and so they wish for his fall.
Still others—the angry
feel so outraged by injuries received
that they long for vengeance
and plan suffering for others.

Everyone perceives vaguely some ultimate good
that will quiet all longing,
and everyone desires it.

If we move toward it with lukewarm love
we correct that deficient love
here on the fourth terrace.

On the three levels above,
greed, gluttony and lust are cleansed,
since too much love was given to those things
which, although good,
are not the essence and root of all good.
Those goods do not give perfect happiness
      to humans.

The human soul,
created eager to love,
is responsive to everything that pleases
as soon as it is roused to action.

Your perception of an object
creates an impression in you
which makes the soul incline toward it.
This inclination is love.
It is a natural feeling,
reinforced in you through pleasure experienced.

Then as fire rises by reason of its form,
which makes it ascend to its natural place;
so too the soul, captivated by desire,
which is a spiritual movement,
never rests until the thing loved
makes it rejoice.

This basic thrust and longing for good
is deep within every human heart,
just as the instinct in bees is to make honey.
This first love deserves neither praise nor blame.

But not every love is praiseworthy in itself,
since some objects only appear good.

Some loves are good or bad,
depending on the object or the intensity of
        our love.
There is innate in us
an ability to discern and judge
which is good or bad.
And besides this we have a noble power:
the freedom of will.
By this inborn liberty
we can choose or reject the objects of our love.

On the fifth ledge of the mountain
the greedy lie on the ground with their
     faces down.

Dante meets a former pope there
who speaks about his sin of avarice:

> Just as our eyes, fixed on earthly things,
> were not lifted on high,
> so justice here sinks them to the earth.
>
> Since avarice
> quenched our love of the true good,
> causing our good works to cease,
> so justice here holds us
> bound, hand and foot.
>
> And as long as the just Lord wishes,
> so long shall we remain
> motionless and outstretched.
>
> Do not kneel before me
> because of the office I once held.
> Get up, brother!
> Do not err:
> I am a fellow servant with you
> and with the others of the one Power.

As Dante moves along the terrace of gluttony, he reflects on the spiritual hunger and thirst within us all:

> The natural thirst,
> that is never quenched
> except by the water requested
> as a grace by the poor Samaritan woman,
> was tormenting me
> and haste urged me on over
> the encumbered way.

On the terrace of gluttony
Dante sees a beautiful, but unattainable, tree
laden with sweet, fragrant fruit.
Beside it is a high rock
from which pure water flows.

He meets an old friend,
who explains how the souls here
suffer hunger and thirst.
The pain heals their former excesses,
transforming their desires
into a joyful willingness to suffer and to love:

> The pain of hunger and thirst
> becomes a solace for us
> since the desire to sacrifice
> brings us to the tree
> which made Christ cry gladly,
>   "My God, My God,"
> when He delivered us with His blood.
> This holy pain weds us again to God.

Before reaching the last terrace
Virgil explains to Dante
how God wonderfully creates
the individual human soul:

> As soon as in the foetus
> the articulation of the brain is perfect,
> the First Mover turns to it with joy
> over such art of nature.
>
> He breathes into it a new spirit,
> replete with powers,
> which draws into itself
> what it finds active there
> and becomes a single soul
> that lives and feels and exists in itself.
>
> To understand this,
> consider the heat of the sun
> which becomes wine when joined with the
>   juice
> that flows from the vine.

On the last terrace lust is purified.
The souls must pass through a wall of fire.

Dante, terrified by this sight, is encouraged by
    Virgil:

> My son,
> here there may be pain, but not death.
> Be assured
> that if you stayed a thousand years in
>   these flames,
> they would not make you lose one hair.

> Put aside all fear
> and enter securely:
> Now see,
> between Beatrice and you is this wall!
> I already see her eyes!
> A bright light
> from the other side of the fire
> called Dante:
> "Come, blessed of my Father."

As Dante and Virgil
reach the summit of the mountain,
the earthly Paradise,

Virgil declares:

> That sweet fruit, happiness,
> which mortals search for on so many
>   branches,
> today will satisfy your hungers.
>
> You have seen the temporal
> and the eternal fires.
> I have brought you here
> with understanding and art.
>
> Now take your own pleasure for your guide.
> You are free from the steep and narrow ways.
>
> See the sun shining on your face;
> see the tender grass,
> the flowers, and the shrubs.
> The fair eyes of Beatrice,
> once in tears, now come rejoicing.
>
> Free upright and whole is your will;
> therefore, I crown and miter you over
>   yourself!

The divine forest of the earthly Paradise,
so dense and green,
gave delight to all the senses.

The gentle breeze made the leaves tremble
while the little birds practiced their art.
The rustling leaves accompanied the singing birds
in a pleasant harmony.

Beside a stream of purest water
a solitary lady went along singing,
picking fresh May flowers
which painted her path.

She seemed to be basking in the rays of love.
Her looks reflected a joyful heart
as she danced along,
gathering red and yellow flowers.

The beautiful woman in love,
Matelda, speaks to Dante:

> You are a newcomer here,
> and you wonder why I smile in this place
> chosen as a nest for the human race.
>
> The reason for my joy
> is found in the words of the psalm:
> "You, O Lord, have delighted me
> by the works of Your hands."
>
> God, the highest good,
> made humans good and for good;
> God gave them this place
> as a pledge of eternal peace.
>
> Through their own fault
> they exchanged innocent laughter and
>   sweet play
> for tears and toil.

Matelda continues:

> You must taste
> the sweet waters of the two streams here
> which flow from God's will:
> the stream of Lethe,
> which wipes away memory of sin,
> and the stream of Eunoe,
> which restores remembrance of good deeds.
>
> The ancient poets sang of this place
> when they dreamed of the Golden Age
> of human happiness.
> Here the root of the human race is innocent;
> here is eternal Spring;
> here is every fruit,
> the nectar of which all the poets sing.

Matelda announces the coming of Beatrice,
who arrives in a burst of splendor,
accompanied by angels and saints.

Beatrice,
the tender lover,
is now the stern judge
who demands from Dante a confession of guilt:

> In your desires for me,
> that led you to love the highest good,
> what chains or pitfalls
> caused you to lose the hope of going
> > forward?

> What comforts or advantages
> were shown on the face of other goods,
> that you sought them?

Dante breaks down
and confesses the detour in his life
away from the love of Beatrice,
who embodies God's truth and goodness:

> The present things
> with their false pleasures
> turned my steps away
> as soon as your mortal face was hidden.
>
> I listened to the alluring sirens
> after your flesh was buried,
> and I forgot you.
>
> Vanities weighed down my wings,
> and I became caught in the snares
> of deceitful things and pleasures.
>
> The novelty of brief enjoyments
> blinded me to your higher beauty.

Beatrice then draws back her veil
and reveals the beauty of her eyes.

Dante exclaims:

> Her eyes are jewels
> from which Love once shot
> His arrows into my heart.
>
> In those two shining emeralds
> are reflected the human
> and divine natures of Christ,
> just as the sun is reflected in a mirror.
>
> What joy and wonder,
> as my soul tasted that food
> which both satisfies and increases hunger!

Beatrice commissions Dante
to take a message back to earth:
that the greatest corruption
of the Church and the State offends God's justice
and God's plan for human happiness.

She directs him:

> Take my words back to those
> who live the life which is a race to death.

> Write and describe how the tree of God's
>   justice
> has been despoiled
> both by the Church and the State.
> These blasphemous acts offend God.

> Carry back this urgent message
> just as a pilgrim from Jerusalem
> wraps his staff with palm branches.

> But be assured that a time will come
> when God will send a savior
> to cleanse the harlot Church
> and her lover, corrupt government.

Dante, after drinking the sacred waters, exclaims:

> I have become born again,
> like young plants renewed by their foliage.

> I am pure and ready to rise to the stars!

H. J. Nawn   *Paradise*

PATH IV.   THE ECSTASY:
Basking in Divine Love

The glory of God
Who moves all penetrates the universe
and shines out in one part more,
and in another less.

    I have been to the heaven
    which receives most of God's light,
    and have seen things
    which one who descends from there
    has neither the skill
    nor the power to relate.

Our mind, as it draws near its desire,
enters so deep
that memory cannot follow it.
Nevertheless,
whatever my mind could treasure of the holy
    kingdom
will now be the subject of my song.

As Beatrice and Dante soar into the heavens,
Dante feels himself being transformed
into a divine state, and exclaims:

> To be "transhumanized"
> cannot be put into words.
> Only You, O Divine Love,
> Who rule the heavens,
> know what this is,
> since it was You
> Who lifted me with Your light.

All things have order among themselves,
and this is the form
that makes the universe like God.

All creatures,
subject in different ways to God's order,
are more or less close to their source.

They move to different ports
over the great sea of being,
each with an instinct given it
that carries it there.

This leads the fire upward toward the moon;
this is the moving force in human hearts;
this binds together and unites the earth.

Thus the Divine Archer
strikes with arrows
not only unintelligent creatures,
but also those with intellect and love.

Beatrice explains to Dante their effortless flight:

The Providence which ordains all this
is the Divine Archer,
Whose power impels us,
aiming us at a joyful target.

You should wonder less at our rising
than at the falling of a stream
from a high mountain to its base.

It would be a marvel if, unhindered,
you should remain settled down below,
as stillness would be in a living flame.

You who lift your hands for the Bread of angels,
on which we feed here below without being sated,
can indeed entrust your vessel to these high seas
and follow the wake of my ship
that singing makes its way,
smoothing the waters ahead of you.

The inborn and perpetual thirst
for the divine kingdom
carries us on almost as fast as
a glance through the sky.

Our desire keeps increasing to see that Being
in which we can see how nature and God are
    united.

Then we will see what we now accept by faith,
not demonstrated,
but as clear and obvious
as the axioms that the human mind assumes.

On the moon
Dante meets the blessed soul of Piccarda,
and asks her if being in the lowest heaven
causes any discontent.

She joyfully responds:

> The power of love quiets our wills
> and makes us wish only for what we have.
> We thirst for nothing else.

> If you consider love's nature,
> you will understand
> that our desires are concordant with
> the will of God Who places us here.

> In this blessed state
> our wills remain within the divine will:
> ours are one with God's.

> In God's will is our peace.
> It is that sea to which all moves,
> both what God and nature create.

Our mind is never satisfied
until that Truth which includes all truth
shines on it.

    Then it comes to its rest
    like a wild animal which reaches its den.
    And it can reach the Truth;
    otherwise, every desire would be vain.

        At the foot of the Truth
        questions and doubts sprout up like
        shoots.

           This is but nature
           pushing us from height to height
           toward the summit.

The greatest gift
that God with bounty bestowed in creating
and the one most conformed to God's own
    goodness,
as well as the one God most prizes,
was freedom of the will.

    All intelligent creatures,
    and they alone,
    are endowed with this supreme gift.

        In establishing a pact of love
        between God and a human person,
        this treasure, the will's freedom,
        becomes the sacrifice by its own act.

Human nature,
when created by its Maker,
was pure and good;
but through its own act
it was banished from Paradise,
since it turned from the way of truth
and from its life.

The human race lay sick down below
for many centuries,
until it pleased the Word of God
to descend.
By an act of God's eternal love
God was united with that human nature
which was estranged from its Maker.

The Divine Person Who assumed our nature
suffered death on the cross,
a death which shook the earth,
opened heaven,
and pleased God.

From the first day of creation
to the last night
there has never been,
nor will there be,
so exalted and magnificent an act!

God was more generous by giving Self
to make humanity able to redeem itself
than if God had merely pardoned it.

Why God chose to redeem us in this way
can be seen only by Those
who have matured in the flames of love.

On the planet Venus
the souls of those who had been notorious
for their erotic love on earth
speak to Dante and Beatrice:

> Here we do not repent but smile,
> not at our faults which we no longer
>   remember,
> but at the Power Who ordained and foresaw.
>
> Here we contemplate
> the art which so much love adorns,
> and we discern the good
> whereby the world below again
> becomes the world above.

Rahab,
once a harlot and pagan
in pre-Christian times,
epitomizes the peace
which the souls on Venus enjoy.
She was taken up
before any other soul
when Christ triumphed over death.

Rahab
was raised to this heaven like a palm branch,
a sign of the great victory won by Christ,
who raised both His palms on the cross.

On the sun,
the greatest minister of nature,
the souls enjoy the brightest light,
since the exalted Father delights them
by showing how He breathes
and how He creates.

Dante becomes so grateful
for this delightful gift of light
that he exclaims:

> All my love was so set on God
> that it eclipsed Beatrice in oblivion.
> This did not displease her;
> she smiled with the splendor
> of her laughing eyes.

Thomas Aquinas,
one of the many splendors
dancing and singing on the sun,
welcomes Dante with this song:

> The ray of grace
> by which true love is kindled,
> and which grows by loving,
> shines so clearly on you
> that it leads you up these stairs
> which no one descends without climbing
> again.
>
> I cannot deny you the wine of my flask
> for your thirst any more than water
> would not flow down to the sea.

The splendid souls on the sun formed a wheel
which moved and sang with a harmony and
     sweetness
unknown except there where joy is everlasting.
Their sweet notes filled my spirit with love.

It was somewhat like the church chimes on earth
which call us, the Bride of Christ,
to rise up and sing matins to our Spouse
Who loves us.

Thomas points out to Dante
two of the bright souls on the sun:

> The Providence
> Who governs the world with that wisdom,
> in which every created vision is vanquished
> before it reaches the bottom,
> in order that the Church,
> the Bride of Him Who espoused her
> with loud cries and with His blessed blood,
> might go to her Beloved secure in herself
> and more faithful to Him,
> ordained two princes to be her guides:
>
> The one, Francis of Assisi,
> was all seraphic in his love;
> the other, Dominic,
> through his wisdom
> was a splendor of cherubic light.

The blessed souls on the sun sing:

> When our flesh, glorious and holy,
> will be clothed on us again,
> our persons will be more acceptable
> for being all complete.

> Then our vision of the Supreme Good will
>   increase
> as well as the ardor of love kindled by it
> and the resultant radiance.

> Like a coal that produces flames,
> but whose white glow shines through them;
> so this brightness which already encircles us
> will be outshone by our flesh,
> which the earth still covers.

The souls on Jupiter enlighten Dante
on God's unfathomable justice:

> The sight that is granted to your world
> penetrates into the Eternal Justice
> as the eye into the sea.

> Near the shore it can see the bottom,
> but out in the open sea it does not see it.

> And nonetheless the bottom is there:
> only the depth conceals it.

"The Kingdom of Heaven suffers violence"
from fervent love and from living hope,
which vanquish the Divine Will.

Not as humans overcome other humans
do they vanquish the Divine Will:
God wills to be overcome;
and, vanquished, God conquers with kindness.

In the heaven of the fixed stars
John the Apostle asks Dante
to declare his love for God,
to state "with how many teeth
this love bites you."

Dante responds:

> All those things
> whose bites can make my heart turn to God
> have concurred in creating my love:
> the existence of the world and my own being,
> the death God suffered so that I might live,
> and the hope that all the faithful share,
> > as I do.

> All these have drawn me
> from the sea of perverse love
> and placed me on the shore of true love.

All the leaves
which cover with foliage
the garden of the Eternal Gardener
I love in proportion to the good
brought to them by God.

In the ninth heaven,
Beatice and Dante gaze on the fixed Point
of dazzling light—God,
the creative center of all life and movement.

In that Point
every *where* and every *when* are centered.
The Eternal Love,
outside of time and every other limit,
opened into new loves,
as it pleased God.

God created
not to acquire any benefit for Self,
but so that God's creation, God's splendor,
might joyfully declare as it shines back:
I subsist, I stand under, I am!

In the final heaven,
the heaven of eternal light,
Beatrice helps Dante
to understand his overwhelming experience:

> We have advanced to the heaven of pure light,
> a light intellectual, full of love;
> a love of the true good, full of joy;
> a joy that transcends all sweetness.
>
> The vivid light that blinds your eyes
> is the greeting with which the Love
> that quiets this heaven welcomes you.
> You are like the candle being prepared
> for its flame.

Dante tries to express the ineffable sight:

> O splendor of God,
> whereby I saw the high triumph of the true
>   kingdom,
> give me power to tell how I saw it!

> There is a light up there
> which makes the Creator visible to all the
>   creatures
> who, only in seeing God,
> have their peace.

In the form of a white rose
the holy company,
which Christ with His blood made His spouse,
was shown to me.

The angels,
flying while singing the goodness
of Him Who enamors them,
were like a swarm of bees
that descend into the great flower,
adored with so many petals,
and reascend to where their love always dwells.

When they descended into the flower
they bestowed the peace and ardor they had
acquired.

The angelic multitude did not obscure
the vision of the souls in the rose,
who directed their loving gaze on one
mark.

As the barbarians from the north were amazed
on seeing the magnificent monuments of Rome,
I too was struck with wonder.

I had come from the human to the divine,
from time to eternity,
from Florence to a people just and sane!

My joy made me content to stand mute:
like a pilgrim,
refreshed in the temple of his vow,
who simply looks
and hopes to report at home how it was.

As Dante approaches the beatific vision of God,
Beatrice relinquishes her role
as guide to Bernard of Clairvaux.

Dante addresses these parting words to her:

> O lady, in whom my hope is strong,
> for my salvation you endured
> to leave your footprints in Hell.
>
> In all the things I have seen
> I acknowledge the grace and power
> of your goodness.
>
> You have lifted me
> from slavery to freedom
> by all those paths,
> by all those means in your power.
>
> Continue your generosity toward me,
> so that my soul,
> which you have made whole,
> may be loosed from the body pleasing to you.

As Dante
gazes on the radiant souls in the white rose,
Bernard directs Dante's eyes to Mary:

> Look now on the face
> which most resembles Christ,
> for only its brightness
> can prepare you to see Christ.
>
> Soon we will direct our eyes
> to the First Love,
> so that looking toward Him,
> you may penetrate as far as possible
> into His brightness.
>
> But first grace must be obtained
> by prayer—grace from Mary,
> who can help you.

Bernard then addresses this tender prayer to Mary:

> Virgin Mother,
> daughter of your Son,
> humble and exalted,
> more than any creature,
> goal established by the Eternal Counsel!
>
> You are the one
> by whom human nature was so ennobled
> that its Creator
> did not disdain to become its creature.
>
> Within your womb was rekindled the Love
> through whose warmth this flower
> has blossomed in eternal peace.
>
> Here you are for us
> a noonday torch of charity,
> and down below among mortals
> you are a living fount of hope.

Lady,
you are so great and so powerful,
that whoever wants grace
and does not turn to you
would have his desire fly without wings.

Your loving-kindness
not only helps those who ask,
but many times freely anticipates the
    request.

In you is mercy;
in you is pity;
in you munificence;
in you whatever goodness
can be found in creatures is resumed.

This man, who has come
from the lowest pit of the universe,
now begs for the grace
to be able to lift his eyes
toward the ultimate salvation.

Dante attempts to describe the ultimate vision:

> My vision was greater than our speech,
> which fails at such a sight,
> just as memory is overcome by excess.
>
> I am like one
> who has seen clearly in a dream:
> the feeling impressed remains afterward,
> but nothing else comes back to mind.
>
> My vision almost wholly fades away,
> and yet the sweetness of it
> is still distilled within my heart.
> Thus in the sunlight the snow melts away.

By an abundant grace
I fixed my eyes on the Eternal Light,
and in its depths I saw contained,
bound by love in one single volume,
what is scattered on leaves throughout the world.

All things fused together in such a way
that what I tell is but a single light.
I believe
I saw the universal form of this knot
because in telling this I feel my joy increase.

Within the deep, clear subsistence
of the great Light
three circles of three colors
and one magnitude appeared to me.

The one, the Son,
seemed reflected from the other,
the Father, as rainbow by rainbow.
And the third, the Spirit,
seemed fire breathed forth equally from both.

O Eternal Light—in Thee alone—Father,
you are;
Son, you know and are known;
Spirit, you love and smile!

The circle of reflected light
seemed depicted with our human image within
        itself.
I desired to see how our image was conformed
to the divine circle
and has a place in it.

But my own wings were not enough for that,
except that my mind was illuminated
by a flash of grace
by which its wish was realized.

Here power failed my lofty imagination.
Yet my desire and my will
were turning in harmony
like a wheel that is moved evenly
by the Love
Who moves the sun and the other stars.

OTHER BOOKS IN THE
MEDITATIONS WITH™
SERIES

HILDEGARD of BINGEN
JULIAN of NORWICH
MEISTER ECKHART
NATIVE AMERICANS
MECHTILD of MAGDEBURG

Bear & Company
Santa Fe, New Mexico